VOYAGERS 1&2
Robots In Space

By Ruth Radlauer and Carolynn Young

A Radlauer Geo Book

AN ELK GROVE BOOK

CHILDRENS PRESS®
CHICAGO

**Created for Childrens Press
by Radlauer Productions, Incorporated**

The authors are grateful to Ellis D. Miner, Ph.D.,
Voyager Deputy Project Scientist, Jet Propulsion Laboratory,
Pasadena, California, for authentication of the manuscript.

Photo credits:
NASA, Jet Propulsion Laboratory, cover and all pages (Artists:
Donald E. Davis, page 18; Ken Hodges, page 38)

Cover:
Separate pictures of the Voyager spacecraft, Jupiter, and its four
largest moons have been combined to make one picture.

Library of Congress Cataloging-in-Publication Data

Radlauer, Ruth.
    Voyagers 1 & 2: robots in space
    (A Radlauer geo book)
    "An Elk Grove book."
    Includes index.
    SUMMARY: Discusses Voyager's space exploration
mission, how the spacecraft conducts experiments using
scientific instruments, and discoveries revealed about
Jupiter, Saturn, and Uranus.
    1. Project Voyager—Juvenile literature.
[1. Project Voyager. 2. Outer space—Exploration]
I. Young, Carolynn. II. Title. III. Title: Voyagers 1
and 2. IV. Title: Voyagers one and two. V. Series
TL789.8.U6V528   1987   919.9'204   86-29922
ISBN 0-516-07840-2

1 2 3 4 5 6 7 8 9 10 11 12 13 14 15 R 93 92 91 90 89 88 87

CONTENTS

20407

The Sun, its nine **planets**, and the **asteroid** belt are shown in this drawing of the **solar system**. The lines were drawn to show **orbit** paths for each planet.

REACH FOR THE PLANETS

Among the billions of stars in the Milky Way **Galaxy**, our solar system is but a tiny speck. Smaller still were the people of the planet Earth who watched eight wandering lights in the night sky. They could only dream of learning more about those other planets in the solar family.

In recent years, still not ready for space travel, Earthlings launched small spacecraft which first orbited the Earth. Later, other craft landed on the Moon and were soon followed by six manned vehicles. Also during this time, more advanced spacecraft gave us our first close-up views of the planets Mercury, Venus, and Mars.

Pleased with the trips around our closer solar neighborhood, we humans then wanted to go out and explore the giant outer planets, Jupiter, Saturn, Uranus, and Neptune, to answer our many questions. Did Jupiter have rings we hadn't seen yet? Were there storms in Saturn's **atmosphere**? Did the planets Uranus and Neptune have additional moons orbiting them?

The millions of miles that separated Earth from those distant worlds made such a journey seem impossible until the positions of the outer planets actually helped us.

planet	body that revolves around a star
asteroids	thousands of objects much smaller than planets, mostly circling the Sun between Mars and Jupiter, but also as close to the Sun as Mercury to almost as far away as Uranus
solar system	the Sun, planets, moons, asteroids, comets, and all the space among them
orbit	(verb) go around on a path; (noun) path followed by a moon around a planet or a planet around a star
galaxy	large group of stars held together by gravity and separated from other galaxies
atmosphere	gases surrounding a planet, moon, or star

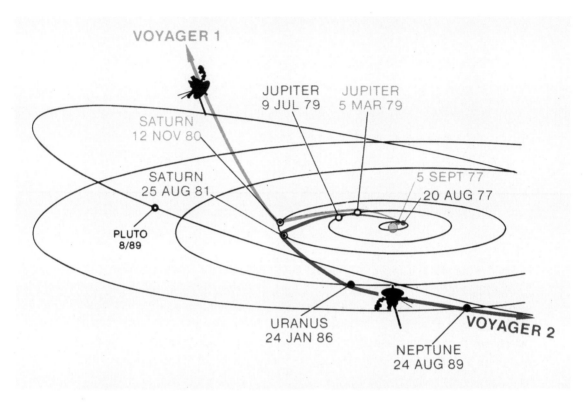

VOYAGER 1

JUPITER
9 JUL 79

JUPITER
5 MAR 79

SATURN
12 NOV 80

SATURN
25 AUG 81

5 SEPT 77

20 AUG 77

PLUTO
8/89

URANUS
24 JAN 86

NEPTUNE
24 AUG 89

VOYAGER 2

The dates of every planetary **encounter** are shown in this
diagram of the Voyager 1 and 2 **trajectories** through the solar
system.

THE VOYAGER PROJECT

Scientists knew that every 175 years the outer planets, Jupiter, Saturn, Uranus, Neptune, and Pluto, are in an almost straight line from Earth. **Engineers** at **NASA's Jet Propulsion Laboratory (JPL**) saw this lineup as a way to plan a *grand tour* of the giant outer planets. By carefully aiming a spacecraft at a close, but safe, distance from each planet, that planet's gravity could capture the spacecraft, increase its speed, and "sling" it on toward the next planet.

The Pioneer 11 spacecraft successfully used this method to fly by Jupiter and Saturn in the 1970s. The Pioneers paved the way for the most ambitious planetary space mission undertaken until that time—the Voyager Project.

The twin Voyagers 1 and 2 each carried 11 science instrument "packages" to study Jupiter and Saturn, several of their moons, and hundreds of millions of miles of space between the planets. After encounters with Jupiter and Saturn, as well as a good look at Saturn's most interesting moon, Titan, Voyager 1's trajectory would then take it up out of the **ecliptic** to travel in an unexplored part of the solar system. Voyager 1 would have no further planetary encounters. If Voyager 2 was healthy after encounters with Jupiter and Saturn, it would continue on to Uranus and Neptune. A flyby of the planet Pluto was not possible because both spacecraft would be headed in directions away from Pluto.

encounter	time when a spacecraft is close to a planet or moon
trajectory	flight path
engineers	in this case, people who designed and built the Voyager spacecraft
NASA	National Aeronautics and Space Administration, a part of the U.S. government
Jet Propulsion Laboratory, JPL	part of California Institute of Technology that explores the solar system for NASA—See *NASA*
ecliptic	imaginary surface upon which the planets orbit the Sun

This life-size model of the Voyager spacecraft is on display at JPL (Jet Propulsion Laboratory).

ROBOTS IN SPACE

The people who built the Voyager spacecraft knew the craft would have to travel greater distances and for a longer period of time than any previous space machine. So the two Voyagers were designed to be the most automatic and independent robots ever sent to explore the planets.

Each Voyager is about the size of a small car and weighs almost one ton. Its most noticeable feature, the large white radio **dish antenna**, is 12 feet across. This antenna provides the all-important two-way radio link between the Earth and the spacecraft. The antenna is always pointed toward Earth except during trajectory corrections and when the spacecraft is maneuvered to perform certain tests and scientific observations.

Tiny onboard **nuclear power plants** provide electricity used to operate several thousand electronic parts. Sixteen **gas jets** around the main body of the spacecraft are fired to stabilize the vehicle or change its position or direction.

The brains of the Voyager spacecraft are six interconnected, onboard computers. Sets of instructions sent from Earth allow the computers to operate the spacecraft as well as the science instruments for days or weeks at a time. Since it takes time for signals from the craft to reach Earth, the computers have often found and corrected problems before mission engineers were aware of them.

dish antenna	device through which radio signals are transmitted and received
nuclear power plant	device that uses heat from nuclear energy to generate electricity
gas jet	small, cone-shaped vent from which gas is released— The gas release steers or maneuvers the craft. See top picture, page 40.

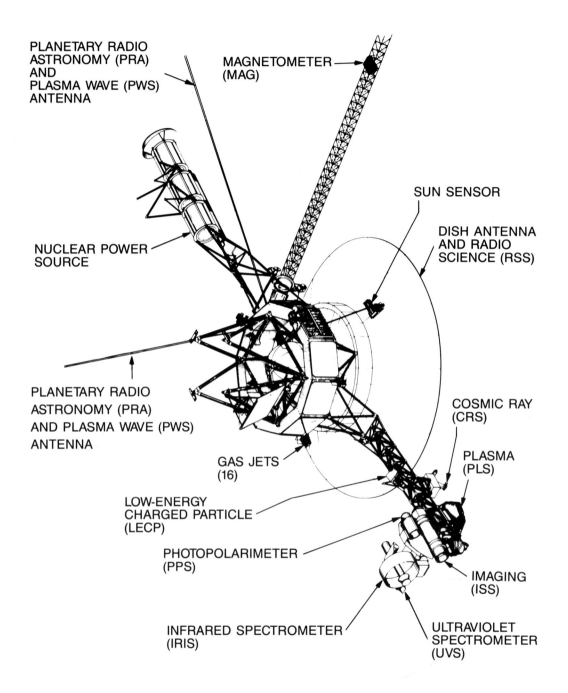

PLANETARY RADIO
ASTRONOMY (PRA)
AND
PLASMA WAVE (PWS)
ANTENNA

MAGNETOMETER
(MAG)

SUN SENSOR

DISH ANTENNA
AND RADIO
SCIENCE (RSS)

NUCLEAR POWER
SOURCE

PLANETARY RADIO
ASTRONOMY (PRA)
AND PLASMA WAVE (PWS)
ANTENNA

COSMIC RAY
(CRS)

PLASMA
(PLS)

GAS JETS
(16)

LOW-ENERGY
CHARGED PARTICLE
(LECP)

PHOTOPOLARIMETER
(PPS)

IMAGING
(ISS)

INFRARED SPECTROMETER
(IRIS)

ULTRAVIOLET
SPECTROMETER
(UVS)

NASA selected the science instruments many years before the
Voyagers were launched. About 130 scientists from the United
States, Europe, Canada, and New Zealand are part of the
Voyager team.

SCIENCE INSTRUMENTS

Eleven science instrument "packages" ride on each Voyager to tell us what's there in the outer solar system. They can be divided into two types: those that point at objects and those that don't. All the pointables except the *RSS*, the Radio Science Subsystem, are mounted on an arm that moves up and down and turns in an almost complete circle.

Two pointing instruments are the *ISS*, or Imaging Science Subsystem, and the *PPS*, the Photopolarimeter. These two instruments detect visible light, the light humans can see. The ISS has two televisionlike cameras which are the "eyes" of the spacecraft. They take **images** of the planets, moons, and rings. The PPS tells us the texture of things like a moon surface or rings. PPS does this by measuring how light changes when it's reflected from or absorbed by these objects.

The *IRIS*, or Infrared **Spectrometer**, and the *UVS*, or Ultraviolet Spectrometer, point at objects to detect levels of red and violet light which cannot be seen by human eyes. The IRIS measures temperatures and, like the UVS, reveals the gases present in planetary or moon atmospheres. The UVS also detects **auroras** in planetary atmospheres.

The RSS conducts experiments using the spacecraft's radio **transmitter**. These experiments help to calculate atmospheric temperatures and determine number, width, and shape as well as the thickness of planetary rings. RSS even lets us find out the size of the materials that make up the rings.

image	likeness or picture of an object
spectrometer	instrument that measures the brightness of light of many different colors
aurora	electrical event that appears in the night sky as streamers, arches, or bands of light
transmitter	device used to send radio signals

(Top) Science instruments are attached to a Voyager spacecraft by engineers at JPL's Spacecraft Assembly Facility.

(Bottom) Each Voyager spacecraft has as many electronic parts as nearly 2,000 color television sets.

The other six instruments do not point at objects, but sample the **environment** around the spacecraft. They operate not only during an encounter, but also while the two spacecraft travel between planets.

The *PRA*, or **Planetary Radio Astronomy**, instrument is similar to a **radio receiver** and "listens" for radio energy from the Sun and the planets.

The *CRS*, or **Cosmic Ray**, the *LECP*, or **Low-Energy Charged Particle**, and *PLS*, or **Plasma**, instruments measure the **solar wind** and other charged particles in space. They estimate how many particles surround the spacecraft and how fast the particles are traveling.

The *MAG*, or Magnetometer, determines whether a planet has a *magnetosphere*, an invisible bubble around some planets that traps charged particles and deflects the solar wind. The *PWS*, or Plasma Wave, instrument is also similar to a radio receiver and gathers information on the behavior of particles within a magnetosphere.

Most of the instruments are wrapped in "blankets," partly to protect them from impact by small particles, but mainly to keep them from getting too cold.

environment	conditions surrounding the spacecraft
planetary radio astronomy	science that uses antennas to detect and measure radio energy from planets and stars
radio receiver	instrument that "hears" radio signals transmitted to it
cosmic rays	high-energy particles that travel through space almost at the speed of light—These often come into the solar system from elsewhere in the galaxy.
low-energy charged particles	particles that contain lower energy than cosmic rays
plasma	charged particles, usually with very low energies, that travel together in streams
solar wind	particles that constantly stream out from the Sun to distances beyond all the planets, and are almost everywhere within that space

Though Voyager 1 was launched 16 days after Voyager 2, its greater speed caused it to pass Voyager 2 while both were traveling in the asteroid belt.

THE JOURNEY BEGINS

Many Voyager engineers, scientists, and their families were among the thousands of people who gathered at Cape Canaveral, Florida, to watch the Voyager launches in the late summer of 1977. Large and powerful Titan/Centaur rockets boosted the Voyagers away from Earth's gravity. Propelled to speeds of about 25-30,000 miles per hour, the Voyagers began the long journey to Jupiter.

Soon after launch, one of the cameras on Voyager 1 was turned around for a parting look at Earth. The resulting picture is the first one ever to show the Earth/Moon system together in the same frame.

But many unforeseen events soon frustrated mission engineers. As sometimes happens with very complicated machines, the Voyagers developed serious problems. Voyager 2's main radio receiver failed. The backup receiver, though faulty, has been used ever since. Some of the science instruments and other moving parts did not operate properly. The sensitive, onboard computers signalled problems later found to be nonexistent.

Here on Earth, JPL engineers used an identical mock-up model of the Voyager to find solutions to these and other problems. By radio, they sent many careful adjustments to the spacecraft over a period of several months. Eventually, Voyager engineers learned to command the spacecraft in ways that actually made both Voyagers better machines than when they were launched.

NASA's Deep Space Communications Complex in Australia has four **tracking stations**. The dish antenna of the largest station is over 200 feet across.

THE DEEP SPACE NETWORK

Mission engineers must maintain constant contact with the spacecraft in order to send instructions that tell the computers what to do. They also need to make sure the instructions are carried out properly and all systems are operating correctly. For this purpose the Voyager Project uses tracking stations at the three locations that make up NASA's Deep Space Network (DSN).

Located in remote areas of California, Spain, and Australia, each location is equipped with three or more tracking stations (steerable dish antennas). As the Earth rotates, each location takes its turn tracking the spacecraft for about eight hours.

The antennas have to be very sensitive to lock onto the signals from the spacecraft. The onboard transmitters send weak signals with only 23 watts of power, less energy than that of the light bulbs used in most refrigerators.

At almost two billion miles away, the Uranus encounter presented a big problem because less **data** could be sent back from Voyager 2 due to the weakness of the signal. Some of the most important Uranus data would be received while the DSN stations in Australia were tracking the spacecraft. NASA received permission from the Australian government to use a large antenna located 200 miles from that country's DSN stations. The borrowed antenna and three of the DSN antennas in Australia were electronically hooked up to make one big antenna, and the important data were successfully received.

tracking station one of several steerable dish antennas at each of three points on Earth, used to track Voyagers 1 and 2, as well as other spacecraft from the U.S. and other countries

data information, usually in the form of numbers

An artist's painting shows Voyager 2 several hours after its
encounter with the planet Neptune and its larger moon, Triton.
The spacecraft will be aimed at a point within several thousand
miles of both Neptune and Triton.

FINDING THE WAY

The Voyager **navigators** *guide* the craft across hundreds of millions of miles to the outer planets. In addition to aiming the spacecraft at close but safe distances from the planets, navigators must make sure the spacecraft reach their destinations when the Voyagers can come close to as many moons as possible.

To estimate where the spacecraft are located way out there in space, navigators use the antennas of the Deep Space Network to conduct certain tests. They send a radio signal to the spacecraft, and the Voyager returns it immediately. Then the navigators measure the difference in **frequency** between these two parts of the signal to find out how fast the spacecraft is traveling. Voyager's distance from Earth is determined by measuring the amount of time it takes for a radio signal to travel from the tracking station to the spacecraft and back.

Just as ancient travelers used stars to guide them on their journeys, navigators also use stars to help them guide the Voyagers. If necessary, the spacecraft's trajectory can be changed to keep it on course. Stars are also used after an encounter to measure actual flyby distances. These measurements help scientists to interpret data accurately.

At Uranus encounter, almost two billion miles from Earth, the navigation accuracy was correct to within ten miles. This amazing accomplishment is equal to sinking a basketball shot from a point halfway around the world.

navigator   person who controls the flight path of the Voyager spacecraft
frequency   number of wave crests per second in a radio signal

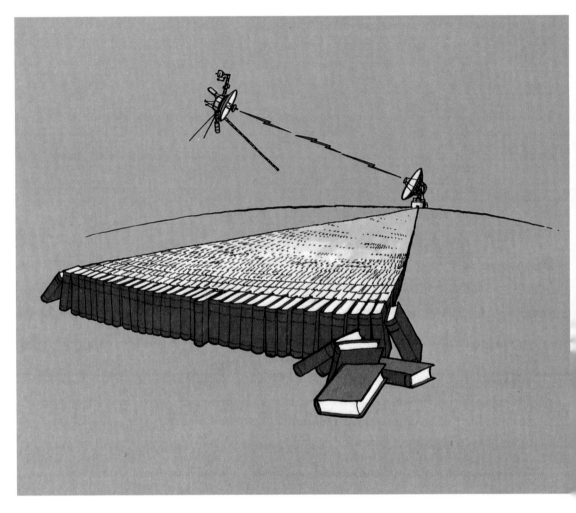

Since launch, both Voyagers have returned enough science data to fill 5,000 sets of the *Encyclopedia Brittanica*.

CRUISE

During the long journey, before the Voyagers encountered each planet, people on the Project were very busy.

Scientists representing each of the 11 onboard instruments formed Science Working Groups to discuss each planet the Voyagers would encounter. Each group made a list of science objectives—the special things about the planets, moons, or rings the group wanted to study during encounters.

Through the many months and years, scientists and engineers developed an observation plan to accomplish the science objectives. Each observation had to be designed for minimum usage of the onboard computers, the least amount of moving of the **scan platform** (for pointable instruments), and the shortest amount of time to do the observation. A detailed sequence of events listed the order in which observations and engineering tests would be performed.

The navigators often checked to make sure the spacecraft were heading toward the correct *aimpoint*—the close but safe distance from the planets and moons.

Shortly before each encounter, all the people working on the Voyager Project went through Test and Training—special classes and tests to prepare them for the upcoming period of high activity. Many were assigned to work night instead of day shifts because encounter operations would continue around the clock.

Of the pointable instruments, only the UVS was kept on during **cruise**, but the others were turned on and tested often. The UVS uses cruise periods to observe ultraviolet radiation from various stars. The CRS, LECP, MAG, and PLS also gather data during cruise.

scan platform   movable arm on which pointing instruments are mounted
cruise   time when Voyagers are traveling between encounters and several instruments are shut down because they're not needed

Jupiter's *Great Red Spot* is a spectacular sight, whether viewed in natural or **enhanced color**. The top image is in natural color, while the colors red and blue in the bottom image have been greatly enhanced, or exaggerated.

HOW PICTURES ARE MADE

The cameras on each Voyager are something like one you may have used. One big difference is that your camera takes pictures recorded on film. Voyager cameras create pictures, or images, the way a television camera does. The darkest dark to the lightest light shades each cause different electrical signals which can either be immediately radioed to Earth or recorded on tape for later sending.

The various dark to light signals are radioed to Earth in the form of numbers. These numbers are fed into a computer at JPL, and an image is produced based on the numbers.

Each Voyager camera has a selection of filters through which images are taken. A clear filter lets in all existing light. Violet, blue, orange, and green filters allow only light in those colors to pass through to the camera. To make a color picture, an object is imaged (photographed) several times, using several different color filters. A very specialized computer at JPL combines the different images into one color picture.

If you have ever taken a picture from a moving car, it probably came out blurred. Voyager cameras face the same problem, but to make matters even worse, the object being imaged is also moving. Voyager engineers developed a plan. While the cameras are focused on a moon where smear could be a big problem, the spacecraft is commanded to roll at a speed that matches as closely as possible the motion of the moon. This technique has eliminated most of the smear from images taken.

enhanced color   computerized technique that exaggerates color to make details clearer for study

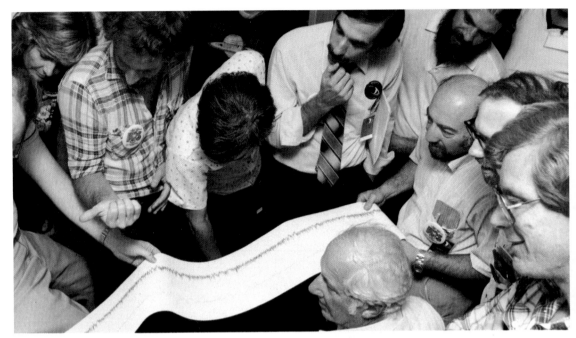

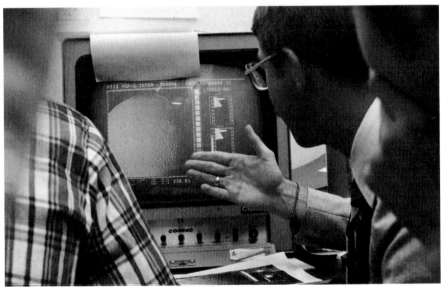

(Top) Voyager scientists, engineers, and members of the press gather around for a first look at Saturn data from the PPS instrument.

(Bottom) ISS scientists examine the first close-up image of Saturn's moon, Enceladus. The **monitor** is hooked up to a special computer that allows more detailed study of interesting features.

ENCOUNTER EXCITEMENT

For the **Voyager Flight Team**, the word *encounter* has several different meanings. It means hard work, excitement, working late, surprises, missed meals, learning, and more hard work. That's because encounter is the busy period during which the Voyagers made their closest approaches to Jupiter, Saturn, and Uranus.

But not all of the high activity took place at JPL. During encounters, the spacecraft themselves were in constant operation as the science instruments took turns making observations. Instructions from onboard computer programs were so precise that not one second was wasted.

Hundreds of people at JPL gathered around monitors to watch as pictures and other information reached Earth. At last, after months and years of detailed planning and work, Flight Team members felt very proud and lucky. Theirs were among the first human eyes to see those faraway worlds as seen by the Voyager cameras.

During encounters, scientists reported their findings at daily **press conferences** with reporters from all over the world. Some things were unusual and mysterious. Views of Jupiter's moon, Io, gave us fantastic surprises. Reporters heard new facts about Saturn's rings. **Planetary geologists** were stunned when they saw images of Uranus' moon, Miranda.

Even though the encounters were exhausting, everyone was sorry when each one was over.

monitor	televisionlike device that displays pictures and other information returned from the spacecraft
Voyager Flight Team	everyone who works on the Voyager Project
press conference	meeting with news reporters to tell findings and answer questions
planetary geologist	in this case, scientist who studies the solid matter of a celestial body, such as a moon

Voyager 1 cameras imaged Jupiter every 96 seconds over a
100-hour period to make a movie of the giant planet. The movie
helped scientists determine that Jupiter's Great Red Spot rotates
once in six days.

ENCOUNTER WITH JUPITER

Voyager 1 was first to encounter the enormous planet named after the ancient Roman god, Jupiter, lord of the heavens. Larger than all the other planets and moons combined, Jupiter is bigger than 1,300 Earths!

The RSS and IRIS instruments confirmed Earth-based studies that had shown Jupiter is an enormous ball of gas, mostly made of **hydrogen** and **helium**. Voyager cameras imaged the cloud tops of Jupiter's dense atmosphere that extends down for thousands of miles to what scientists believe is a **molten** center about the size of the Earth.

The Great Red Spot in the southern hemisphere is Jupiter's most noticeable feature. Voyager images verified that it is a raging storm about the size of six Earths.

Jupiter is a place of high activity and extremely fast motions. The planet rotates almost two and a half times as fast as the Earth. The dark bands and white zones of clouds move in eastward and westward directions at speeds of up to 300 miles per hour. Voyager made images of enormous bolts of lightning on the dark side of the planet. They are much larger and more powerful than **superbolts** found in Earth's atmosphere.

A surprising Voyager discovery was that Jupiter is a ringed planet. The ring had not been seen through Earth-based **telescopes** because the ring particles are very tiny and were simply lost in Jupiter's brightness.

hydrogen	simplest, lightest gas known
helium	second lightest gas known
molten	liquified by heat; not solid
superbolt	extremely bright and powerful lightning bolt
telescope	arrangement of tubes and glass lenses (or mirrors) that makes it possible to see distant objects more clearly

(Top) Although Jupiter's moon Io is actually a yellow-green, this image of it with its exaggerated color became known as "the pizza picture." The circular feature in the center turned out to be part of an exciting discovery about Io.

(Bottom) A **mosaic** shows that Jupiter's moon Callisto is a world of **craters**.

With his first telescope **Galileo** gazed upon Jupiter and also found the four largest of Jupiter's icy moons. Io, Europa, Ganymede, and Callisto are called the *Galilean* moons after their discoverer.

Io, the Galilean moon closest to Jupiter, really put on a show for the Voyager cameras. As the spacecraft flew by, Io surprised us with nine erupting volcanoes! Io is the only moon known to have active volcanoes.

Voyager showed that Europa, the smallest and brightest of the Galileans, is the smoothest of all known bodies in the solar system. There are no high peaks or deep valleys. Dark streaks on its surface appear to be cracks which have been filled in with darker material from inside the moon.

Ganymede, the largest moon in the solar system, has a puzzling surface. Some parts are dark and old-looking with many **impact craters**. Other areas are cleaner and brighter. These places have fewer impact craters, yet many ridges and valleys are present. These differences suggest that Ganymede's surface has moved around the way Earth's continents have moved.

Callisto, the darkest of the Galileans, is twice as bright as Earth's Moon. Its ancient surface is peppered with craters from **meteorite** impacts that probably happened when the solar system was still very young.

Images from both Voyager encounters confirmed the discovery of three additional moons, making a total of 16 known moons orbiting Jupiter.

mosaic	single picture made by pasting many smaller ones together
crater	See *impact crater*.
Galileo	Galileo Galilei, Italian astronomer who discovered the moons of Jupiter in 1610
impact crater	bowl-shaped depression formed by the force of an object striking the surface
meteorite	particles, sometimes very large, that strike the surface of a planet or moon

Saturn is shown with a picture of Earth that was taken during one of the manned flights to the Moon. Saturn is as big as 763 Earths!

ENCOUNTER WITH SATURN

Voyager's long-awaited encounter with Saturn began in the autumn of 1980. Voyager 2 would arrive nine months later. What awaited them?

Like Jupiter, Saturn is a gigantic gaseous planet made mostly of hydrogen and helium. It is the second largest planet in the solar system. The PRA instrument determined that Saturn rotates in 10 hours and 39 minutes. Saturn's journey around the Sun takes more than 29 years. Though it is very big and heavy, this planet's **density** is less than that of water. If placed in a large enough body of water, Saturn would actually float!

With its soft yellow color and dazzling rings, Saturn looks like a very peaceful place. But Voyager images showed turbulent storm features in its atmosphere similar to but smaller than those on Jupiter. The strongest winds were found near the **equator** with wind speeds of up to 1,100 miles per hour mostly in an easterly direction.

Voyager scientists were surprised and confused when they saw close-up views of the rings. The four or five rings, observed through Earth-based telescopes and by the Pioneer spacecraft, are actually made of thousands of ringlets or strands. What's more, the billions of pieces of icy ring material vary in size from small dust particles to boulders as big as an average house.

density   mass per unit volume—A cup of water has less density than a cup of lead.

equator   imaginary line around the middle of a planet which is an equal distance from the north and south poles

Saturn's moon, Mimas, has a huge impact crater named Herschel. The crater is 80 miles wide and six miles deep. The peak at the center of Herschel is almost as high as Earth's Mount Everest.

Voyager images revealed at least three additional moons orbiting Saturn, increasing the total to at least 17 known moons. The two Voyager encounters gave Earthlings a close look at all 17 of these moons.

The biggest moon, Titan, is the second largest moon in the solar system, and the only one with a very dense atmosphere. This moon is especially interesting because its atmosphere makes Titan very similar to what Earth was before it became **habitable** for humans. Although the atmosphere prevented the Voyager cameras from imaging Titan's surface, the IRIS instrument and RSS measurements told us that Titan is very cold, about $-289°$ Fahrenheit *(below zero.)*

Mimas, Enceladus, Tethys, Dione, and Rhea are **spherical** in shape. They are composed mostly of water ice, and have many impact craters.

Enceladus is the brightest of the Saturnian moons because it reflects almost 100% of the sunlight that hits it. Some parts of its surface are smooth and uncratered. Scientists believe those parts of Enceladus have been **resurfaced** within the past 100 million years.

Iapetus is truly strange. One half is jet black, and the other half is almost pure white.

Hyperion's irregular, battered shape shows a history of meteorite impacts, some powerful enough to knock off pieces of this moon.

The outermost of the known moons, Phoebe orbits Saturn in a direction opposite to that of all the other moons. Its orbit direction, small size, and dark color suggest that Phoebe may be an asteroid captured by Saturn's gravity.

habitable   able to sustain life
spherical   round in shape, like a ball
resurfaced   having developed a new surface, perhaps by some unknown process that heats the inside and causes the surface to soften and smooth out

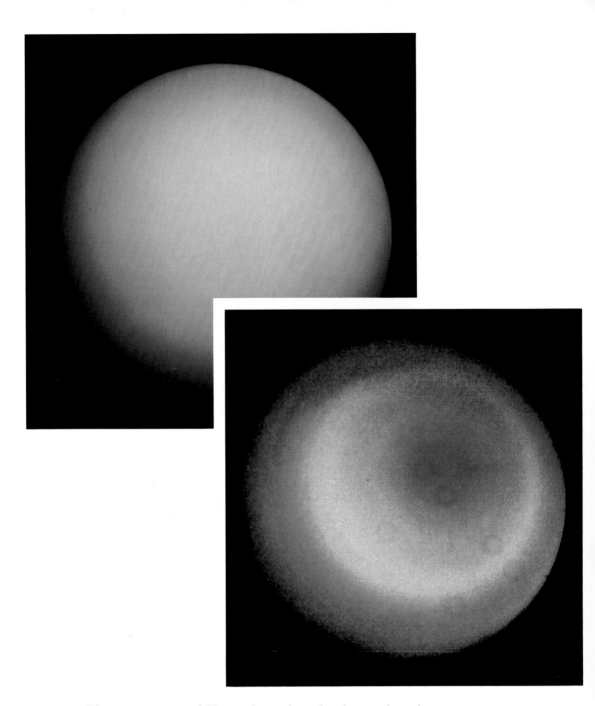

The top image of Uranus' south pole shows the planet as a human would see it if perched on the spacecraft. When **false color** was added to the bottom picture, it revealed what may be polar haze or smog. The doughnut-shaped features were caused by dust specks on the camera's lens.

URANUS ENCOUNTER

Voyager 2 traveled almost 8½ years and two billion miles to give Earthlings their first close-up views of Uranus. No other spacecraft from Earth had ever visited the third largest planet in the solar system.

All planets in the solar system, except Uranus and Pluto, have their equators more or less parallel with the ecliptic. Uranus is different because it's tipped on its side, causing its south pole to point just below the ecliptic. Scientists wonder if this extreme tilt was caused by an Earth-size object colliding with Uranus many, many years ago.

Uranus is made mostly of hydrogen, helium, and **methane**. The methane gas causes it to be light aqua in color. When the Sun's light falls on Uranus, the methane absorbs all of the red light waves, causing Uranus to radiate in a mixture of blue and green light.

Images of Uranus were less exciting than those of Jupiter and Saturn. Because Uranus is colder than Jupiter and Saturn, most of its clouds form deep in the atmosphere where Voyager cameras couldn't see them.

During the same year the Voyagers were launched, astronomers studying Uranus noticed that light from a distant star was blocked nine times as the planet passed in front of it. Further study confirmed that a system of rings had been discovered around Uranus. Their existence was known only because they had interrupted starlight, for the nine thin rings are dark as coal. Even the Voyager cameras couldn't see the rings very well until the spacecraft made its closest approach to the planet. It was then, though, that the tenth and eleventh faint rings were discovered, as were ringlets or strands of dust that look much like Saturn's rings.

false color computerized technique that substitutes one color for another to make details clearer for study

methane gas containing hydrogen and carbon, commonly known as swamp gas

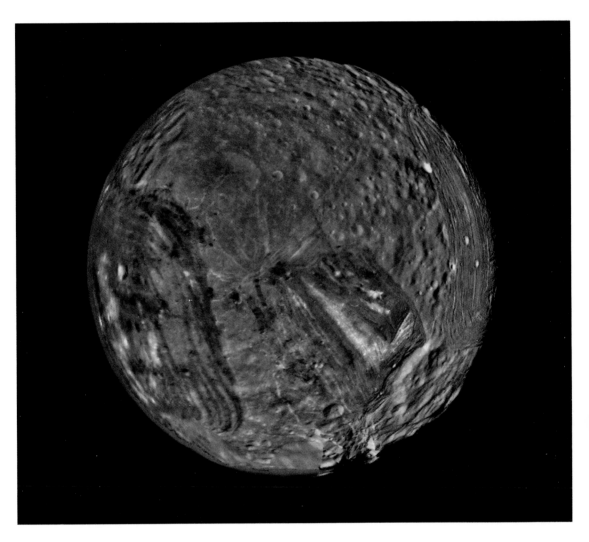

The Uranian moon, Miranda, gave Voyager scientists their most exciting images. Craters, ten-mile-high cliffs, deep valleys, and trenches were discovered by Voyager 2.

As Voyager 2 approached Uranus, the number of known moons quickly increased. In addition to the five previously known moons, ten new ones were found.

The icy moons, Oberon, Titania, Umbriel, Ariel, and Miranda, were discovered between 1787 and 1948. The largest, Oberon and Titania, are about half the size of Earth's Moon. The ten newly discovered moons are very small and dark, with **diameters** of 100 miles or less.

The surfaces of the moons, Ariel, Titania, and Oberon, have undergone many changes as a result of impact craters and deep **incisions**. Some of these features are filled with a bright frostlike material which appears to have welled up from the interior. Oberon has a huge mountain towering nearly four miles.

The moon Umbriel is quite puzzling. Its dark gray, bland surface suggests that Umbriel hasn't changed much since it was formed. That might not seem strange, but why is Umbriel's **terrain** undisturbed when it's located between Ariel and Titania, two moons with surfaces that have experienced many changes?

Miranda was the most shocking of all the Uranian moons. Its surface appears to contain just about every type of terrain known to planetary geologists. Some regions suggest that liquid flowed on Miranda at some time in its past. One gigantic cliff is nearly 12 miles high, twice as high as a jet airliner flies above Earth. Voyager scientists cannot explain why Miranda has such a different geological past from that of the other Uranian moons.

diameter	length of a straight line through the center of a circle or sphere from one side to the other
incision	cut, like an earthquake fault
terrain	land shapes such as valleys, craters, mountains

Educated guesses have led scientists to think that Triton, Neptune's larger moon, may look like this artist's conception that shows shallow lakes of liquid **nitrogen** on a surface partially covered by methane ice.

ON TO NEPTUNE

Twenty days after the Uranus encounter, several of Voyager 2's gas jets were **ignited**. For three hours, the thrusting energy of the jets slowly adjusted the trajectory. At the end of the maneuver, Voyager 2 was on course for its encounter with the planet Neptune on August 24, 1989.

At nearly 2.8 billion miles from the Sun, Neptune is truly on the outskirts of the solar system. While it is the fourth largest planet in the solar system, Neptune cannot be seen from Earth with the naked eye. Even today's powerful telescopes have given little new information about the bluish-green planet since it was discovered in 1846. But recent Earth-based observations show that Neptune may have a partial ring system, with rings that don't go all the way around the planet.

Triton and Nereid are Neptune's two known moons. Triton is about the same size or larger than Earth's Moon, and may have a thin atmosphere. Nereid is only 200 miles in diameter. Since its orbit is the most highly **eccentric** of any known moon, scientists believe Nereid may be a captured asteroid or comet.

Voyager 2 may solve some of these mysteries when it flies near both Neptune and Triton. Those encounters will probably be the closest flybys that Voyager 2 has had. It seems a fitting way to celebrate the 12th anniversary of the Voyager launches with a last swing-by on the historic grand tour of the four giant outer planets.

nitrogen   colorless, tasteless, odorless gas that makes up 78% of Earth's atmosphere and is present in all living tissue
ignited   fired up
eccentric   not circular, but changing in distance from the center

(Top) Each Voyager carries a gold-plated, copper record that bears a message about our world. This follows the example set by the Pioneer 10 and 11 spacecraft. They carried small metal plaques with similar information. (Notice the cone-shaped gas jet that was mentioned on page 9.)

(Bottom) Unless found by other intelligent beings, the Voyagers will travel forever within the Milky Way Galaxy that is similar to this spiral galaxy in the **constellation** Pisces.

GREETINGS FROM EARTH

After their missions are completed, both Voyagers will eventually leave our solar system. As they enter the realm of **interstellar space,** they will become ambassadors from Earth. Some day, maybe hundreds or thousands of years from now, curious space travelers may intercept one of our Voyagers and wonder what it is. What messages would you want to deliver to them? Many people pondered this question and here is what they decided.

A gold phonograph record along with a needle for playing it was attached to each Voyager spacecraft. Scientific drawings on the record's cover show how the 90-minute record can be played.

The record begins with 118 pictures that can be changed from sound signals to visual images. The first pictures would help future viewers learn the size and position of Earth in comparison with the Sun and other planets. Illustrations show different sizes, weights, and ages of Earthlings. Many pictures show people working, eating, laughing, and relaxing together. Special attention is given to families.

Next are friendly messages spoken in 54 languages, followed by sounds of humans, animals, and machinery. The rest of the record contains several kinds of music which we hope shows we have feelings and how we express some of them.

Because of the immense distances that separate the stars, the Voyager spacecraft will probably *not* be found by other intelligent beings. But if any beings ever do listen to our gold record, they will know that the people of Earth thought of them and wanted to say, "Hello."

constellation area of the sky with well-defined groups of stars visible from Earth

interstellar space space between stars

GLOSSARY

asteroids   thousands of objects much smaller than planets, mostly circling the Sun between Mars and Jupiter, but also from as close to the Sun as Mercury to almost as far away as Uranus

atmosphere   gases surrounding a planet, moon, or star

aurora   electrical event that appears in the night sky as streamers, arches, or bands of light

charged particles   See *low-energy charged particles.*

constellation   area of the sky with well-defined groups of stars visible from Earth

cosmic rays   high-energy particles that travel through space almost at the speed of light—These often come into the solar system from elsewhere in the galaxy.

crater   See *impact crater.*

cruise   time when Voyagers are traveling between encounters and several instruments are shut down because they're not needed

data   information, usually in the form of numbers

density   mass per unit volume—A cup of water has less density than a cup of lead.

diameter   length of a straight line through the center of a circle or sphere from one side to the other

dish antenna   device through which radio signals are transmitted and received

eccentric   not circular, but changing in distance from the center

ecliptic   imaginary surface upon which the planets orbit the Sun

encounter   time when a spacecraft is close to a planet or moon

engineers   in this case, people who designed and built the Voyager spacecraft

enhanced color   computerized technique that exaggerates color to make details clearer for study

environment   conditions surrounding the spacecraft

equator   imaginary line around the middle of a planet which is an equal distance from the north and south poles

false color   computerized technique that substitutes one color for another to make details clearer for study

frequency	number of wave crests per second in a radio signal
galaxy	large group of stars held together by gravity and separated from other galaxies
Galileo	Galileo Galilei, Italian astronomer who discovered the moons of Jupiter in 1610
gas jet	small cone-shaped vent from which gas is released—The gas release steers or maneuvers the craft. See top picture, page 40.
habitable	able to sustain life
helium	second lightest gas known
hydrogen	simplest, lightest gas known
ignited	fired up
image	likeness or picture of an object
impact crater	bowl-shaped depression formed by the force of an object striking the surface
incision	cut, like an earthquake fault
interstellar space	space between stars
Jet Propulsion Laboratory, JPL	part of California Institute of Technology that explores the solar system for NASA—See *NASA*
low-energy charged particles	particles that contain lower energy than cosmic rays
methane	gas containing hydrogen and carbon, commonly known as swamp gas
meteorite	particles, sometimes very large, that strike the surface of a planet or moon
molten	liquified by heat; not solid
monitor	televisionlike device that displays pictures and other information returned from the spacecraft
mosaic	single picture made by pasting many smaller ones together
NASA	National Aeronautics and Space Administration, a part of the U.S. government
navigator	person who controls the flight path of the Voyager spacecraft
nitrogen	colorless, tasteless, odorless gas that makes up 78% of Earth's atmosphere and is present in all living tissue

nuclear power plant	device that uses heat from nuclear energy to generate electricity
orbit	(verb) go around on a path; (noun) path followed by a moon around a planet or a planet around a star
planet	body that revolves around a star
planetary geologist	in this case, scientist who studies the solid matter of a celestial body, such as a moon
planetary radio astronomy	science that uses antennas to detect and measure radio energy from planets and stars
plasma	charged particles, usually with very low energies, that travel together in streams
press conference	meeting with news reporters to tell findings and answer questions
radio receiver	instrument that "hears" radio signals transmitted to it
resurfaced	having developed a new surface, perhaps by some unknown process that heats the inside and causes the surface to soften and smooth out
scan platform	movable arm on which pointing instruments are mounted
solar system	the Sun, planets, moons, asteroids, comets, and the space among them
solar wind	particles that constantly stream out from the Sun to distances beyond all the known planets, and are almost everywhere within that space
spectrometer	instrument that measures the brightness of light of many different colors
spherical	round in shape, like a ball
superbolt	extremely bright and powerful lightning bolt
telescope	arrangement of tubes and glass lenses (or mirrors) that makes it possible to see distant objects more clearly
terrain	land shapes such as valleys, craters, mountains
tracking station	one of several steerable dish antennas at each of three points on Earth, used to track Voyagers 1 and 2, as well as other spacecraft from the U.S. and other countries
trajectory	flight path
transmitter	device used to send radio signals
Voyager Flight Team	everyone who works on the Voyager Project

INDEX

THE AUTHORS

Carolynn Young's interest in space exploration began in 1976 when she saw a televised press conference about the findings of the Viking Mission to the planet Mars.

It was a dream come true when she joined the administrative staff of the Voyager Flight Science Office at JPL six months after the Voyager launches. She was among the fortunate few to see the first close views of Jupiter, Saturn, and Uranus. While encounters are going on, Carolynn schedules interviews between members of the press and Voyager's chief scientists. During cruise periods of the Voyager journey, Carolynn gives public lectures and answers many letters to JPL from people all over the world. Carolynn lives in Pasadena, California.

Ruth Radlauer has written of matters celestial before. Along with Dr. Charles Stembridge, she wrote *PLANETS* and *COMETS*. She is the author of 20 books about the national parks as well as co-author with her husband of more than 150 other books ranging in subjects from Volcanoes to Gymnastics and Rock Climbing to Robots. Ruth and her son Dan collaborate on the creation of musicals for young people to perform. The Radlauers live in La Habra Heights, and Idyllwild, California.